Novena Outside

Opening Hymn

Invocation

All kneel

Let us unite with Christians of all ages in praising Mary and committing ourselves to her powerful protection.

All **We fly to your patronage, O holy Mother of God, despise not our petitions in our necessities, but deliver us from all dangers, O glorious and blessed Virgin.**

Pray for us, O holy Mother of God.

All **That we may be made worthy of the promises of Christ.**

Let us pray.

All **Lord Jesus Christ, you have given us your Mother, Mary, to be our Mother, ready at every moment to help us: grant, as we pray before her image and call on her help, that we may always be faithful to the graces that are ours through your death and resurrection. May the life they bring us be to your glory on earth and our eternal happiness in heaven! Amen.**

Scripture

The Magnificat

Let us now praise and thank God in the words placed on Mary's lips:

All **My soul glorifies the Lord,**
my spirit rejoices in God, my Saviour.
He looks on his servant in her lowliness;
henceforth all ages will call me blessed.

The Almighty works marvels for me.
Holy his name!
His mercy is from age to age,
on those who fear him.

He puts forth his arm in strength
and scatters the proud-hearted.
He casts the mighty from their thrones
and raises the lowly.

He fills the starving with good things,
sends the rich away empty.

He protects Israel, his servant,
remembering his mercy,
the mercy promised to our fathers,
to Abraham and his sons for ever.
Glory be to the Father...

Let us pray.

All **Holy Mother of God, Virgin ever-blessed, O Mary Immaculate, pray for us, intercede for us, do not refuse to help us. We are confident, and know for certain, that you can obtain all you will from your Son, our Lord Jesus Christ, the King of ages, who lives with the Father and the Holy Spirit, for ever and ever. Amen.**

Sermon

Petitions and thanksgivings are announced.

Prayers for this Novena

Lord Jesus Christ, at a word from Mary, your Mother, you changed water into wine at Cana of Galilee. Listen to your people gathered here to honour our Mother of Perpetual Succour. Grant our petitions and accept our humble thanks.

All **O Mother of Perpetual Succour, we call upon your most powerful name. You are the safeguard of the living and the salvation of the dying. Your name will always be on our lips, especially in time of temptation and at the hour of our death. Your name is confidence and power. Blessed Lady, help us whenever we call on you. We will not be satisfied with merely pronouncing your name. Our daily lives will proclaim that you are truly our Mother of Perpetual Succour.**

Remember, O most Blessed Virgin Mary, that never was it known that anyone who fled to your protection, implored your help, or sought your intercession, was left unaided. Filled, therefore, with confidence in your goodness, I fly to you, Virgin of Virgins, my Mother. To you I come, before you I stand, sinful and sorrowful. Mother of the Word Incarnate, despise not my petitions, but in your mercy hear and answer me. Amen.

You have been made for us, O Lady, a refuge,

All **a helper in need and tribulation.**

Let us pray.

All **Almighty and merciful Lord, you have given us to venerate the picture of your most blessed Mother under the special title of Perpetual Succour. Graciously grant that, amidst the changes of our journey through life, we may be so defended by the continual protection of the same Immaculate ever-Virgin Mary that we may deserve to obtain the rewards of your eternal redemption, who live and reign with the Father and the Holy Spirit, world without end. Amen.**

For the intentions of our Holy Father the Pope:

Our Father; Hail Mary; Glory Be.

Hymn

Mary, let perpetual succour
  be the answer to our prayer,
for thy Son, of all the wretched
  gives to thee perpetual care.
Ever ready help hast thou,
  let thy children feel it now.

Though we try to rise yet ever
  down in misery we fall;
so like feeble children sadly,
  for our Mother's help we call.
Ever ready help hast thou,
  let thy children feel it now.

Blessing and Prayer for the Sick

Let us pray.

All **O Lord, look upon your servants labouring under bodily weakness. Cherish and revive the souls you have created so that, purified by our sufferings, we may soon find ourselves healed by your mercy through Christ our Lord. Amen.**

The priest extends his right hand towards the sick

May the Lord Jesus Christ be with you that he may defend you, within you that he may sustain you, before you that he may lead you, behind you that he may protect you, above you that he may bless you. In the name of the Father and of the Son and of the Holy Spirit. Amen.

Benediction

Eucharistic Hymn

Either the following, or some other suitable hymn will be sung.

O salutaris hostia,
quae coeli pandis ostium,
bella premunt hostilia,
da robur, fer auxilium.

Uni trinoque Domino
sit sempiterna gloria,
qui vitam sine termino
nobis donet in patria. Amen.

Prayer to the Blessed Sacrament

All **My Lord Jesus Christ, who, for the love you have for us, remain night and day in this Sacrament, full of compassion and love, awaiting, calling and welcoming all who come to visit you, I believe you are present in the Sacrament of the Altar. I adore you from the depth of my nothingness, and I thank you for all the graces you have bestowed upon me, especially for having given me yourself in this Sacrament, for having given me your most holy Mother Mary as my advocate and for having called me to visit you in this church. My Jesus, I love you with all my heart. I am sorry for having offended your Infinite Goodness. I am resolved never more to offend you for the time to come, and now, although unworthy, I give myself completely to you. I renounce my own will, my affections, my desires and all that I possess. From now onwards do you dispose of me, and all that I have, as you please. All I ask of you and desire is your holy love, final perseverance and the perfect fulfilment of your will. Amen.**

St Alphonsus Liguori

Pause for silent prayer.

Tantum Ergo

Tantum ergo Sacramentum
 veneremur cernui:
et antiquum documentum
 novo cedat ritui:
praestet fides supplementum
 sensuum defectui.

Genitori, genitoque
 laus et jubilatio,
salus, honor, virtus quoque
 sit et benedictio:
procedenti ab utroque
 compar sit laudatio. Amen.

Therefore, we before him bending
 this great Sacrament revere:
types and shadows have their ending,
 for the newer rite is here;
faith, our outward sense befriending,
 makes our inward vision clear.

Glory let us give, and blessing,
 to the Father and the Son,
honour, might and praise addressing,
 while eternal ages run;
ever, too, his love confessing
 who, from both, with both is one. Amen.

You have given your people bread from heaven *(Alleluia).*

All **The bread which is full of all goodness *(Alleluia).***

God, who in this wonderful Sacrament has left us a memorial of your passion, help us so to reverence the sacred mysteries of your Body and Blood that we may always experience in our lives the effects of your redemption; who live and reign for ever and ever. Amen.

Divine Praises

All **Blessed be God.**
Blessed be his Holy Name.
Blessed be Jesus Christ, true God and true man.
Blessed be the name of Jesus.
Blessed be his most Sacred Heart.
Blessed be his most Precious Blood.
Blessed be Jesus in the most holy Sacrament of the Altar.
Blessed be the Holy Spirit, the Paraclete.
Blessed be the great Mother of God, Mary most holy.
Blessed be her holy and Immaculate Conception.
Blessed be her glorious Assumption.
Blessed be the name of Mary, Virgin and Mother.
Blessed be St Joseph, her spouse most chaste.
Blessed be God in his angels and in his saints.

Final Hymn

Novena During Mass

Responsorial Psalm

All My soul glorifies the Lord,
my spirit rejoices in God, my Saviour.
He looks on his servant in her lowliness;
henceforth all ages will call me blessed.

The Almighty works marvels for me.
Holy his name!
His mercy is from age to age,
on those who fear him.

He puts forth his arm in strength
and scatters the proud-hearted.
He casts the mighty from their thrones
and raises the lowly.

He fills the starving with good things,
sends the rich away empty.

He protects Israel, his servant,
remembering his mercy,
the mercy promised to our fathers,
to Abraham and his sons for ever.

General Intercessions

We ask Mary to join with us, as we turn to God in prayer, calling to mind our needs, the needs of the Church and of all God's people.

Response **May the Virgin Mary intercede for us.**

For ourselves: that we may have courage in our troubles. ***R.***

For our families: that our homes may be places of welcome, love and understanding. ***R.***

For our parish: that we may use our talents in the service of the Church. ***R.***

For the Church: that she may be blessed with good priests and religious. ***R.***

For the whole world: that God's Kingdom of justice, peace and joy may flourish everywhere. ***R.***

For our own personal intentions: we pray for a few moments in silence. ***R.***

The Novena Prayer

Together let us say the Novena Prayer.

All **O Mother of Perpetual Help, with the greatest confidence we come before your holy picture to be inspired by the example of your life. We think of you at that moment, when, full of faith and trust, you accepted God's call to be the mother of his Son. Help us, your children, to accept with joy our calling in life.**

When you learned that your cousin, Elizabeth, was in need, you immediately went to serve her and offer your help. Help us, like you, to be concerned with others.

We think of you, Mother, at the foot of the Cross. Your heart must have bled to see your Son in agony. But your joy was great when he rose from the dead, victorious over the power of evil.

Mother of Sorrows, help us through our trials and disappointments. Help us not to lose heart. May we share with you and your Son the joy of having courageously faced up to all the challenges of life. Amen.

Prayer of Thanksgiving

This prayer is said after Mass, at the Shrine of Our Lady.

All **O God, our Creator, we thank you for the gift of life and all the gifts of nature: our senses, our faculties, our talents and our abilities. We thank you for creating us in your image and likeness and for giving us this earth to use and develop, to respect and cherish.**

Despite our failures, you continue to show your love for us today by increasing the life of your Spirit within us at the Eucharistic table.

Finally, Father, we thank you for giving us Mary, the Mother of your Son, to be our Mother of Perpetual Help, and for all the wonderful things you have done for us, especially for giving us your Son, Jesus, to be our Redeemer.

We are grateful for all the favours we have received through her intercession. We pray that those past favours may inspire us to greater confidence in your loving mercy and in seeking the aid of our Mother of Perpetual Help. Amen.

Hymns

Holy Virgin, by God's decree,
  you were called eternally;
that he could give his Son to our race.
  Mary, we praise you, hail full of grace.

Ave, ave, ave, Maria.

By your faith and loving accord,
  as the handmaid of the Lord,
you undertook God's plan to embrace.
  Mary, we thank you, hail full of grace. *Ave...*

Joy to God you gave and expressed,
  of all women none more blessed,
when in mankind your Son took his place.
  Mary, we love you, hail full of grace. *Ave...*

Refuge for your children so weak,
  sure protection all can seek,
problems of life you help us to face.
  Mary, we trust you, hail full of grace. *Ave...*

To our needy world of today
  love and beauty you portray,
showing the path to Christ we must trace.
  Mary, our mother, hail full of grace. *Ave...*

As I kneel before you,
as I bow my head in prayer,
take this day, make it yours
and fill me with your love.

Ave Maria, gratia plena,
Dominus tecum, benedicta tu.

All I have I give you,
ev'ry dream and wish are yours.
Mother of Christ, Mother of mine,
present them to my Lord. *Ave Maria...*

As I kneel before you,
and I see your smiling face,
ev'ry thought, ev'ry word
is lost in your embrace. *Ave Maria...*

Salve Regina, Mater misericordiae;
vita, dulcedo, et spes nostra, salve.
Ad te clamamus, exsules filii Hevae,
ad te suspiramus, gementes et flentes
in hac lacrimarum valle.
Eia ergo, advocata nostra, illos tuos
misericordes oculos ad nos converte;
et Jesum, benedictum fructum ventris tui,
nobis post hoc exsilium ostende.
O clemens, O pia, O dulcis Virgo Maria.

Hail, Queen of heav'n, the ocean star,
guide of the wanderer here below;
thrown on life's surge, we claim thy care;
save us from peril and from woe.
Mother of Christ, star of the sea,
pray for the wanderer, pray for me.

O gentle, chaste and spotless maid,
we sinners make our prayer through thee;
remind thy Son that he has paid
the price of our iniquity.
Virgin most pure, star of the sea,
pray for the sinner, pray for me.

And while to him who reigns above,
in Godhead one, in Persons three,
the source of life, of grace, of love,
homage we pay on bended knee,
do thou, bright Queen, star of the sea,
pray for thy children, pray for me.

Immaculate Mary! Our hearts are on fire,
that title so wondrous fills all our desire.

Ave, ave, ave Maria!

We pray for God's glory, may his kingdom come!
We pray for his vicar, our father and Rome.

Ave...

We pray for our mother, the Church upon earth,
and bless, sweetest Lady, the land of our birth.

Ave...

Now to God be all glory and worship for aye,
and to God's virgin mother an endless Ave.

Ave...